Options Trading

Take Your Trading to the Next Level With Winning Strategies and Precise Technical Analysis Used by Top Traders to Beat the Odds and Achieve Consistent Profits in the Options Market.

Samuel Feron

Contents

Introduction

Are you a new investor who just got started? Want to master the art of options trading but lack any prior knowledge?

If so, then you should read this book.

You must venture beyond basic transactions and limited stock and exchange-traded fund (ETF) purchases if you wish to succeed in the stock market. If you know what you're getting into and how to practice options trading successfully, options trading can provide a path to significant stock market success.

Options are financial derivatives that offer the holder the right, but not the obligations, to purchase or sell an underlying asset at a particular price, known as the striking price, on or before a given date, known as the expiration date. At this time, the option is valid.

Options are flexible financial tools that can be utilized for income generation, hedging, and speculating. Investors often employ them to reduce risk and increase returns.

This book is intended to introduce options thoroughly and how they work, covering the many types of options, how to buy and sell them, and how to utilize them in different strategies.

This book will help you learn the basics of options and how to utilize them effectively in your financial portfolio, whether a novice or a seasoned investor.

You will get knowledge about several trading strategies to use as well as some potential dangers. When you finish reading this book, you'll have a solid foundational understanding of options trading and whether it fits you.

Chapter One

Introduction To Options Trading

You're not the only one if you've recently joined the options trading bandwagon. In fact, with 7.47 billion contracts exchanged in 2020, the popularity of trading in options, or contracts that let you wager on which way you believe a stock price is headed, reached a record high. The Options Clearing Corporation reports a 52.4% rise from the previous year.

Options trading is rapidly expanding as both experienced and novice investors embrace it. These two groups are starting to understand the freedom options offer: investors can lock in a stock price without acquiring it.

Trading options can greatly increase your income, reduce your risk, and protect yourself from market volatility. Options can complement stocks in your portfolio for these reasons. Investors have more options when they trade both than when they trade equities alone. Options can function almost like an insurance policy. For instance, buying specific options might help offset any possible losses on your shares if the value of a company you hold declines.

Options may allow you to change your strategy without selling your stock, lower your breakeven point, and even establish a purchase price for a stock below its current market value.

Despite its widespread appeal, options trading is not that simple, and getting started requires a lot of forethought. We break down below what active investors need to understand before trying options.

What Are Options?

An option is a contract that grants you the right to purchase or sell a financial product for a predetermined amount of time at the agreed-upon price.

Equities, indexes, and ETFs are just a few financial products with options available. Options are referred to as "derivatives" because their value is "derived" from the underlying asset.

You trade ownership in a corporation when you trade stocks. In contrast, the possibility or obligation to buy or sell the underlying stock is traded when options contracts are bought or sold. The mere possession of an option does not grant the holder ownership of the underlying securities or any dividend rights.

Why Trade Options?

Options have been available for more than 40 years, but they have only begun to receive the attention they merit. Many investors have ignored options because they are too complex and difficult to understand. Because neither they nor their brokers received adequate training on utilizing options, many more people have had initial negative experiences with them. Like any strong tool, options can be misused to cause serious issues.

Finally, the financial media and certain well-known personalities in the market have mistakenly associated the word "risky" or "dangerous" with options. The individual investor should consider both sides of the argument before deciding on the worth of options.

Option options may offer an investor four main benefits, in no particular order. With benefits like these, it is understandable that individuals who have been utilizing options for some time would be perplexed as to why they are not more well-liked. Let's examine each of these benefits individually.

Cost-Efficiency

Options have a lot of leverage. As a result, an investor can acquire an option position comparable to a stock position while saving a ton of money. For instance, an investor would need to shell out $16,000 to buy 200 shares of an 80-dollar stock. The total cost, however, would only be $4,000 if the investor bought two $20 calls, each representing 100 shares (2 contracts x 100 shares/contract x $20 market price). After that, the investor would have an extra $12,000.

It is not nearly that easy. The investor must choose the best call to acquire to duplicate the stock position. However, this tactic, usually referred to as stock replenishment, is feasible and economical.

Lower Risk, When Used Properly

There are instances where purchasing options are riskier than holding stocks, but there are other circumstances where using options can help lower risk. It all relies on how you employ them. Due to the lower financial commitment required, options might be less risky for investors than shares and are more resistant to the potentially disastrous impacts of gap openings.

Options are safer than stocks since they are the most reliable type of hedging. A stop-loss order is commonly issued to safeguard the position when an investor buys equities. The stop order is intended to halt losses below a certain price that the investor has specified. These orders have difficulty because of the way they are written. A stop order is implemented when the stock moves at or below the limit specified in the order.

Greater Chance Of Returns

You don't need a calculator to understand that if you spend less money while earning about the same profit, your % return will be larger. Options often offer to investors when they are paid off.

More Strategic Options

Options also provide extra investing possibilities, which is its final significant benefit. Options are an incredibly adaptable tool. Options can be used in a variety of ways to replicate various positions. These positions are referred to as synthetics.

Synthetic positions give investors several options for achieving the same financial goals, which can be beneficial. Although synthetic positions are regarded as an advanced option issue, options also present a wide range of additional strategic choices. For instance, when an investor wishes to short a stock, many investors use brokers who charge a margin. The price associated with this margin need may be very high. Other investors work with brokers who categorically forbid shorting stocks. Investors are effectively handcuffed and forced into a world of black and white while the market trades in color because they cannot play the downside when necessary. However, no broker regulation prohibits investors from buying puts to play the downside, making this a clear advantage of trading options.

The investor can trade in the market's "third dimension" or lack of direction using options. Options allow the investor to trade not just changes in stock prices but also time and volatility changes. Most of the time, stocks don't make significant changes. The few equities that do move dramatically do so rarely. Your capacity to capitalize on stagnation may be the difference between realizing your financial goals and keeping them as distant aspirations. Only choices provide the tactical options required to succeed in any market.

Risks Of Options Trading

Thousands of fresh investors opened brokerage accounts after the pandemic. Sadly, few purchased quality equities to hold onto them; instead, they experimented with high-risk, high-reward tactics like options trading. If you intend to trade options, you must know all the associated risks.

Buying and selling contracts based on the value of an underlying asset, like a stock, bond, commodity, or currency, is a high-risk investing strategy known as options trading. Due to its potential for significant profits and capacity to provide leverage, it appeals to many investors. However, Options trading comes with several risks that, if not properly managed, can result in severe losses.

Investors should be informed that options trading can be risky and there is a chance of losing money. The possibility that an investor would be exposed to more risk than they can handle is one of the major risks of trading options. Investors must be sure they understand the risk they are taking on and have the financial resources to pay their losses because the leverage obtained by using options can magnify both gains and losses.

Trading options also involve a liquidity risk. The investor might be forced to honor the contract and incur a loss if they cannot find a buyer or seller in time. Additionally, when expiration draws near, the time value of options contracts declines, which can further diminish the value of the investor's position.

The potential for mispricing is the third risk associated with trading options. It is conceivable for the market to be mispriced, resulting in unanticipated losses for the investor, given that the pricing of options contracts depends on intricate mathematical models. Option contract pricing is also open to speculation, which increases the risk of sudden, significant price changes.

Finally, counterparty risk is a risk associated with options trading. This is the danger that the other party to the deal won't carry out their end of the bargain, costing the investment money. Investors must ensure they only trade with reputable brokers or exchanges governed by the appropriate authorities if they want to protect themselves from this.

In conclusion, trading options can be profitable, but big risks are involved. Before trading, investors must know the risks involved and have the money to cover any potential losses. To prevent mispricing and unforeseen losses, investors must also ensure they are trading with trustworthy brokers or exchanges and know about the pricing of options contracts.

Chapter Two

Understanding The Options Market

From a simple approach to detailed, complex trades, you can use various options trading strategies. However, betting on rising prices is generally done by trading call options, and betting on dropping prices is done by trading put options.

Option buyers and sellers must exchange at least 100 shares of stock or other assets. However, there is no requirement to exercise options if a deal doesn't make money. Investors will only lose the price they paid to buy the contracts if they decide not to exercise their options. Consequently, trading options can be inexpensive to speculate on various asset types.

What Are The Different Types Of Options?

If you're an investor looking for short-term financial instruments, option is perfect for you. It is a derivative contract that grants the owner the authority to purchase or sell securities within a predetermined time frame at an agreed price. Call and Put options are the widely-known even though several options are available on the stock market.

Call Option

Simply put, a call option implies a "right to buy." It gives the contract's owner the choice to buy a stock at the decided-upon strike price at any time up until or on the day the contract expires. When the market is bullish, an investor will buy this option because they believe the stock's market price will increase in the future. By exercising the option and buying the shares at the striking price, which is less expensive than the current market price, the option holder can benefit as the stock price increases.

Put Option

On the contrary, a Put option grants the owner the "right to sell." Within the expiration term, a put holder may sell the option as stock at a strike price. A put option is placed when an investor anticipates a future decline in the market's price (a bearish market). The Put holder can sell the asset at the strike price, higher than the current market price, as the underlying asset's price decreases in the open market. As a result, the investment is successful.

Understanding The Essentials Of Option Prices

Options contracts give the buyer or investor the right, but not the obligation, to buy and sell a security at a predetermined price known as the striking price. Options contracts trade on options exchanges and have an expiration date known as an expiry. Because they draw their value from the underlying security or stock price, options contracts are considered derivatives.

The buyer of an equity call option will want the underlying stock price higher than its strike price by the time it expires. Conversely, a put option buyer would prefer that the underlying stock price is below the put option strike price by the time the contract expires.

Numerous variables affect the cost of an option's premium and, ultimately, the feasibility of an options contract. The following two elements are the most crucial in deciding whether an option is profitable when called in the money (ITM) or unprofitable when called out of the money (OTM).

Intrinsic Value

One of the key elements affecting the premium of an option is its intrinsic value. Intrinsic value is the portion of the premium of the price difference between the current stock price and the strike price.

Consider a call option that an investor has on a stock that is now trading at $49 per share. The option's premium is $5, and the strike price is $45. Since the option's strike price was increased by $4 since it was established, $4 of the premium's $5 total represents intrinsic value.

The investor in the illustrated case pays the $5 up-front cost and receives a call option that entitles him to buy shares at the $45 strike price. It won't be exercised until the option is profitable or in the money. By adding the premium to the strike price, $5 + $45, we can determine the amount the stock must rise for us to profit: $50. The break-even point is $50, which means that the stock must increase beyond $50 before the investor can benefit (net of broker commissions).

To calculate the portion of an option's premium that is attributable to intrinsic value, an investor would subtract the option's strike price from the stock's current price. Intrinsic value is significant because it increases the likelihood that changes in the price of the underlying stock will have a greater impact on the option's value and profitability. The level of a stock's price movement is known as its volatility.

Assessment Of Intrinsic Value

The term "delta" refers to an option's sensitivity to changes in the underlying stock. Investors should expect the option to move around 60 cents for every buck the stock moves, while a delta of 1.0 indicates that the option will possibly move dollar for dollar with the stock.

The fact that the delta for puts is shown as a negative number illustrates how the link between the put and stock movement is inverse. If the price falls $1 per share, the value of a put with a delta of -0.4 should rise by 40 cents.

Time Value

Time value is the monetary worth attached to the time left before an option expires. The more time value is built into the option's premium, the closer the option's expiration date is.

In other words, time value refers to the fraction of the premium over the intrinsic value an option buyer pays in exchange for the right to possess the contract for a specific time. Time value is hence often referred to as extrinsic value.

If an option has time left until expiration, investors are ready to pay more for it because there is more opportunity to make money. Since investors are ready to pay for that additional time for the contract to become profitable or have intrinsic value, the longer the time left, the higher the premium.

Remember that for an option to have intrinsic value, the underlying stock's price must rise above the strike price. The likelihood that the stock's price will rise over the strike price and into profitability increases with the length of the contract. Because of this, time value is important in determining an option's premium and the possibility that the contract would expire in the money.

Time Decay

As the option expiration date draws near, the time value gradually lowers. An investor's incentive to pay the premium decreases as an option's remaining time decreases since there is less opportunity to benefit from the option. The possibility of making a profit decreases as the option's expiration date approaches, which causes the time value to decrease. Time decay is the process by which the value of time decreases.

During its first half, an options contract typically loses around one-third of its time value. As the option's expiration date approaches, its value falls off increasingly rapidly until it eventually reaches zero.

Investors must consider both time value and time decay when estimating the likelihood that an option will be profitable. There must be enough time left on the option to make a profit if the strike price is far from the current stock price. Determining whether an option has any chance of having intrinsic value requires understanding time decay and the rate at which time value depreciates.

Evaluation Of Time Value

The Greek letter theta represents time value. Theta reduces the premium; thus, option buyers must be adept at market timing. Allowing a profitable trade to sit so long that theta significantly decreases the gains is a mistake many option traders make.

For instance, a trader might purchase an option for $1 and watch it rise to $5. Only $4 of the $5 premium is intrinsically valuable. The option's premium will gradually decrease to $4 at expiration if the stock price doesn't rise any further. Before purchasing an option, a clear exit strategy should be established.

Volatility And Time Value

A stock's volatility, or degree of price swings, also influences the likelihood that an option will expire in the money. If traders anticipate volatility, implied volatility, sometimes referred to as vega, can increase the option premium.

The market's perception of the likelihood that the price of a stock will change is measured by implied volatility. Options traders will ask for a greater price for the options they sell since excessive volatility increases the likelihood that a stock will move past the strike price.

This is why well-known occurrences like earnings often result in lower profits for option buyers than initially anticipated. Even while there is a chance that the stock would move significantly, option prices are typically high before such occurrences, which reduces the potential rewards.

In contrast, option prices tend to decline during periods of extreme calm, making them reasonably priced to purchase. However, the option will remain inexpensive, giving a limited chance for profit until volatility increases again.

Chapter Three

Technical Analysis For Options Trading

Investors and traders often use the popular technical analysis tool to help them decide what to do when trading stocks and options.

Technical analysis provides clearer entry and exit signals for generating money in the markets for many options traders. Technical analysis (when applied correctly) has a lot of empirical evidence to support it as a trustworthy trading technique, even though some investors disregard it as arbitrary and inconclusive.

Any successful trader must be able to utilize technical analysis to its fullest potential. Technical analysis used properly, along with volume analysis, can increase your advantage in every trade.

Understanding that these evaluations are valid even without a key event like a lawsuit or merger and acquisition discussion is crucial.

These ideas make it easier to see trends and reversals, gauge the strength of an asset's momentum, and identify potential support and resistance locations.

Important Technical Indicators For Trading Options

Depending on their trading style and the kind of security they want to trade, traders can use any one of hundreds of technical indicators.

This section focuses on several significant technical indicators well-liked by options traders. In short-term trading, technical indicators are often employed to assist the trader in determining the movement's range (how much), direction (which way), and duration (how long).

The holding term is important since options are subject to time decay. While an options trader is restricted by the small period determined by the option's expiration date, a stock trader can retain a position indefinitely. Given the time limits, momentum indicators—which tend to spot overbought and oversold levels—are well-liked by options traders.

Let's examine a few typical indications that options traders utilize, such as momentum and others.

RSI, Or Relative Strength Index

The relative strength index measures a security's pace and change of price movements to identify oversold and overbought conditions. It is a momentum indicator that contrasts the size of recent profits against recent losses over a given period. The RSI scales from 0 to 100, with values above 70 often suggesting overbought levels and below 30 generally indicating oversold levels.

RSI is more effective for options on specific stocks than indexes since individual equities exhibit overbought and oversold positions more often. For short-term trading based on RSI, highly liquid, high-beta stock options are the ideal prospects.

Bollinger Bands

Bollinger bands are a common tool to evaluate volatility, and all options traders are aware of the significance of volatility. As volatility rises, the bands widen; as volatility falls, they narrow. The likelihood of security being overbought or oversold increases with the distance between the price and the upper and lower bands.

The security may be ready for a reversal if the price moves outside the bands, and options traders can position themselves accordingly. For instance, the trader might open a long put or short call position following a breakout above the top band. On the other hand, a breakout below the lower band would offer a chance to employ a long call or short put strategy.

Additionally, remember that it is often a good idea to sell options during high volatility when option prices are high and to buy options during low volatility when they are more affordable.

Intraday Momentum Index (IMI)

The Intraday Momentum Index is a reliable technical indicator for high-frequency option traders wishing to wager on intraday movements. Indicating overbought and oversold levels, it combines the ideas of intraday candlesticks and RSI to provide a proper range (similar to RSI) for intraday trading. An options trader may be able to identify possible chances using IMI to place a bullish trade during an intraday correction in an up-trending market or a bearish trade during an intraday price bump in a down-trending market.

The IMI is determined by dividing the total of up days by the sum of up days plus the sum of down days, or ISup /(ISup + IS down), and multiplying the result by 100. The most popular time period is 14 days, though the trader can select any number of days. Like RSI, the stock is overbought if the resultant figure exceeds 70. And the stock is regarded as oversold if the outcome is less than 30.

Money Flow Index (MFI)

MFI is a momentum indicator incorporating price and volume information. Also called volume-weighted RSI. A number above 80 indicates that a security is overbought, while a rating below 20 suggests that a security is oversold. The MFI indicator analyzes the entrance and outflow of money into an asset over a specified period (usually 14 days), and it is a sign of "trading pressure."

MFI is more suited to stock-based options trading (as opposed to index-based options trading) and longer-duration contracts because it relies on volume data. A trend change can be anticipated when the MFI goes in the opposite direction of the stock price.

Put-Call Ratio Indicator (PCR)

The put-call ratio compares the trading volume of call and put options. The variations in the put-call ratio's value rather than its absolute value represent a shift in the market's mood.

When more calls are being purchased than puts, the ratio is above 1, which denotes bullishness. When the put volume exceeds the call volume, the ratio is less than 1, which denotes bearishness. The put-call ratio, however, is sometimes viewed by traders as a contrarian indication, leading them to choose to trade against market trends in anticipation of an eventual reversal.

(OI) Open Interest

The open or unsettled contracts in options are indicated by open interest. OI gives clues about the strength of a certain trend but does not always point to a specific uptrend or downturn. A strengthening trend is indicated by dropping open interest, while an increase in open interest signals new capital intake and, consequently, the sustainability of the current trend.

Charting Patterns And Trends

A chart pattern is a shape within a price chart that helps predict what prices may do in the future based on prior performance. Technical analysis is based on chart patterns, which demand traders be fully aware of what they are looking at and searching for.

The most crucial thing to remember when employing chart patterns in your technical analysis is that you are not a guarantee that a market will move in that anticipated direction; rather, they are only a potential outcome for the price of an asset.

Shoulder And Head

A shoulder and head chart pattern has two slightly smaller peaks on either side of a huge peak. To forecast a bullish-to-bearish reversal, traders look for shoulder and head patterns.

The first and third peaks will often be smaller than the second peak, but they will all revert to the same degree of support, or the "neckline," as a result. The third peak is expected to break out into a bearish decline once it has retreated to the level of support.

Double Tops

A double top is another pattern that traders employ to draw attention to trend reversals. An asset's price will often reach a peak before declining to a level of support. Then, it will ascend again before turning around more permanently against the current trend.

Double Bottoms

A double-bottom chart pattern indicates a period of selling that caused an asset's price to fall below a level of support. It will then increase till a point of resistance before declining once more. Finally, as the market turns more positive, the trend will invert and start moving upward.

Because a double bottom signals the conclusion of a downtrend and the beginning of an upswing, it is a bullish reversal pattern.

Rounding Bottom

A rounded bottom chart pattern might indicate both a continuation and a reversal. For instance, an asset's price during an uptrend may decline briefly before rising again. This would continue the positive trend.

An instance of a bullish reversal rounding bottom is when the price of an asset is in a downward trend while developing a rounding bottom before the trend reverses and starts a bullish uptrend.

Traders will attempt to profit from this pattern by purchasing halfway around the bottom, at the low point, then profiting from the continuation after it breaks over a level of resistance.

Cup And Handle

A bullish continuation pattern called the cup, and handle is used to illustrate a period of bearish market sentiment before the general trend finally moves in a bullish direction. The cup resembles a rounding bottom chart pattern, while the handle resembles a wedge pattern, discussed in the next section.

The price of an asset will probably experience a brief retracement after the rounding bottom; this retracement is called the handle since it is limited to two parallel lines on the price graph. Eventually, the asset will break free of the handle and resume its general bullish trend.

Wedges

Wedges develop as the distance between two sloping trend lines for an asset's price changes tightens. There are two types of wedges, namely, rising and falling wedges.

A trend line wedged between two upwardly sloping lines of support and resistance is an example of a rising wedge. In this instance, the support line is steeper than the resistance line. When an asset price breaks through the support level, it usually indicates that the price will decrease more drastically.

A falling wedge happens between two levels that are inclined downward. The line of resistance, in this instance, is steeper than the line of support. A falling wedge typically signals that the price of an asset will increase and pass through the level of resistance.

Rising wedges are reversal patterns that indicate a bearish market while falling wedges indicate a bullish market.

Flags Or Pennants

Pennant patterns or flags are formed after an asset experiences a period of upward movement, followed by a consolidation. In most cases, the trend will begin with a substantial gain before degenerating into smaller upward and downward moves.

Pennants can indicate a continuation or a reversal and be bullish or bearish. Pennants can be viewed in this context as a bidirectional pattern because they exhibit continuations or reversals.

Even though a pennant design resembles a wedge pattern or a triangle pattern, both described in the next sections, it's vital to remember that wedges are thinner than pennants or triangles. Additionally, a wedge is either rising or descending, whereas a pennant is always horizontal, making wedges different from pennants.

Ascending Triangle

The ascending triangle represents the continuance of an uptrend and is a positive continuation pattern. A horizontal line can be drawn along the swing highs, the resistance, and an ascending trend line can be formed along the swing lows, the support, to create ascending triangles.

Ascending triangles often have two or more peak highs that are identical, making it possible to create a horizontal line. The horizontal line denotes the degree of historical resistance for that specific asset, while the trend line represents the pattern's overall upward tendency.

Descending Triangle

A falling triangle, on the other hand, denotes a bearish continuation of a downward trend. A trader typically opens a short position during a descending triangle to profit on a sinking market, maybe using CFDs.

Because descending triangles signify a seller-dominated market, they typically move lower and break through the support, making successively lower peaks more common and unlikely to reverse.

A downward-sloping resistance line and a horizontal line of support indicates descending triangles. The trend will eventually breach the support, and the downward movement will continue.

Symmetrical Triangle

The symmetrical triangle formation can be bullish or bearish, depending on the market. In either case, it is typically a continuation pattern, which indicates that after the pattern has formed, the market will typically keep moving in the same direction as the general trend.

Symmetrical triangles are formed when the price converges with a string of lower peaks and higher troughs. The symmetrical triangle sometimes reveals that there has been a brief period of upward reversals, even if the general trend is bearish.

The market could, however, break out in either direction if there is no discernible trend before the triangular pattern takes shape. As a result, symmetrical triangles are a bilateral pattern and are best applied in choppy markets where it is unclear in which direction the price of an asset will likely move.

Chapter Four

Fundamental Analysis For Options Trading

Along with technical analysis (TA), fundamental analysis is one of the two primary techniques investors employ to uncover profitable investment opportunities for strategies like value investing or growth investing. Here, we will define fundamental analysis, describe its process, and provide examples.

What Is Fundamental Analysis?

Fundamental analysis (FA) is a technique that helps to assess if a security or asset is trading at a discount to its value or a premium. It is often used in stock markets and for bonds, currencies, commodities, and even cryptocurrencies.

FA is based on the theory that market prices might occasionally overvalue or undervalue an asset because they don't consider all important fundamental considerations. Investors take into account various economic and financial elements, including the overall health of the economy, the level of competition, or the financial statements of each asset or security - everything that affects a particular economy.

Finding all of the available data and making inferences about which variables could affect supply and demand are similar to research when determining what might impact the price of a firm's stock or a particular commodity.

How Is Fundamental Analysis Done?

Depending on the method, investors undertake fundamental analysis by either assessing the health of the general economy before focusing on the specific performance of a stock, or vice versa, by examining a specific company's financial performance.

Together with technical analysis (TA), which assumes that market prices accurately reflect all fundamental factors rather than using historical price and volume data to forecast future prices, fundamental analysis is one of the primary techniques used to identify new investment opportunities.

The main objectives of fundamental analysis are to find the asset's fair or intrinsic value and determine whether it is under or overvalued.

The Fundamental Trading Mechanics

A thorough examination of the economy, the sector in which the firm operates, and the company itself form the foundation of the basic method of valuing a company. The trader uses the information from this study to predict market trends and calculate the stock's intrinsic value.

The trader can also use fundamental analysis to evaluate if a stock is undervalued or overvalued and to help anticipate the future value of the stock. Successful analysis can reveal investment opportunities that the market hasn't yet identified and help the trader make a successful investment.

The trader might apply various methodologies while performing a fundamental study on a company. The trader may decide, for instance, to contrast businesses within a given industry with businesses in other industries.

Examples Of Fundamental Analysis In Trading

The success of a trader's application of fundamental analysis depends on various variables. Thinking about the target trade's possible profit is a smart place to start. It's crucial to understand the different ways that fundamental analysis can help in the identification of potentially profitable transactions as well as the reasons behind why such trades might be profitable.

Here are two instances of how fundamental analysis could be used to locate potentially profitable investments.

Established Stocks

Established businesses, mutual funds, and other sizable financial institutions make significant market swings and can help investors build their portfolios. In this situation, a trader's profit will serve as payment for the risks they took.

You can use fundamental analysis in various methods to decide whether an investment in a well-known publicly traded stock has the potential to be profitable. The goal is to weigh every piece of information influencing the stock's price.

Traders will first consider the present economic climate, which includes national and international events that could impact the company and its stock price. For instance, are there any local problems (like wars or labor strikes) that would make it difficult for the business to get the supplies it needs to produce goods? Are macroeconomic issues, such as rising interest rates or inflation, impacting the company's pricing structure? What is the outlook for the business sector as a whole? Are there any disruptive elements that could have a detrimental effect on the company's market niche?

A thorough investigation of the company comes next in a fundamental trading study. It's critical to understand the organization's business model and revenue stream. The company's financial accounts will be reviewed by traders, who will look at the cash flow statements, income statements, and balance sheets going back at least two years. The trader will be looking for obvious signals of growth during this assessment and efficient management that may mitigate any unfavorable macroeconomic circumstances and any competitive advantages the company may have that could spur future growth.

Finally, the trader will do a competitive analysis of the company akin to the fundamental analysis already carried out. The trader will analyze findings for both the target company and its rivals to assess all the companies as viable investments. At this stage of the fundamental examination, the trader may learn that the company has good investment potential or that a rival company has greater potential. Or, after some thought, the trader can decide that none of the studied companies would make good buys right now.

Initial Public Offerings

An initial public offering (IPO) can allow investors to profit from the difference between the price the stock will ultimately settle at and the stock's IPO price. Your profits as a trader serve as payment for the risk you assume.

While many of the fundamental analysis methods described above are available to traders, they might not be sufficient to assess an IPO's potential for profit. Risk concerns may be associated with IPOs that a fundamental analysis cannot account for. For instance, conducting a fundamental analysis for IPOs in relatively new businesses can be difficult because there isn't much historical information available to evaluate and compare.

Additionally, because of extensive media publicity, the price of an IPO stock can occasionally increase. Some investors buy in an IPO without doing their homework and due diligence because they are affected by herd instincts and follow the crowd. This may result in an initially high stock price that falls sharply once trading starts.

Special Considerations

Fundamental analysis is typically not used to make tactical, immediate decisions. The right move can be made at the proper time with the help of technical analysis; however, a fundamental analysis should be used strategically over a longer time frame.

A trader can learn about the market's general health and the attractiveness of a particular security compared to other securities by using fundamental research. To choose when and how to respond to the information obtained through fundamental analysis, some investors prefer to use technical analysis.

Free Goodwill

Dear option trading enthusiast,

Greetings from the fascinating world of options trading! Get ready for a thrilling voyage where you'll negotiate the complexity of the financial markets, harness the power of derivatives, and discover the possibility of substantial rewards.

I want to underline the importance of your feedback as you go through the pages of this book. Future option traders' understanding and success can be significantly influenced by your distinctive perspective, which you have developed through your experiences and insights.

I invite you to write an honest review and share your opinions, feelings, and key takeaways.

Your review is a gift to people about to embark on their option trading endeavors and is more than simply a collection of words. Your insights can motivate, educate, and guide them to make wise choices in this dynamic and ever-changing industry.

Your feedback count, and it's possible that reading one of your reviews will inspire someone else to start their own successful options trading business. Sharing your experiences can motivate and empower people to take calculated risks, develop their skills, and reach their financial goals.

I want to thank you from the bottom of my heart for being willing to add to our collective understanding of option trading. Your review will play a significant role in the legacy of this book, helping future readers and influencing how options trading is understood for years to come.

I appreciate your contribution to our outstanding community. Your knowledge and experiences are priceless, and your contribution will improve aspiring options traders' lives.

I wish you unending success and profitable deals through the fascinating options trading world. Thanks!

Chapter Five

Developing A Winning Options Trading Strategy

When done correctly, trading options are one of the most effective means to build long-term wealth. If you're a newcomer in the stock market or investing, you might not be familiar with Options or Option Trading Strategies. But don't worry—we've got you covered!

In exchange for a premium given by the buyer to the seller, an investor can purchase or sell an instrument, such as a stock or even an index, at a certain price over a predetermined period through an option.

This chapter will cover some of the top option trading strategies that we believe any trader or investor should, at the very least, be familiar with. But first, how do you choose the right strategy for your trading style?

Choosing The Right Trading Strategy

Even if you are an expert in options trading, you won't likely make much money unless you can put that knowledge to use and choose wisely which transactions to enter into and when. Deciding which strategy to employ is the most difficult aspect of planning each transaction.

This is true if you are starting with options trading or don't have a thorough grasp of the many strategies that can be employed. Even seasoned traders occasionally find it difficult to choose the ideal strategy. At the same time, it is true that the more experience you have with options trading, the easier such decisions become.

The truth is that there is no right strategy. There are many things to consider, and a strategy that can be effective in one situation may be unsuitable in another. A lot also depends on the individual because what is right for one trader might not be right for another.

Although we can't guarantee that you'll use the right approach in any given circumstance, we can give you pointers on how to decide for yourself. Here, we examine a few of the factors you should be thinking about.

If you are still learning how to trade options, we advise you to take the time to determine the best approach each time you open a new position. As you gain expertise, your understanding of how each strategy works will improve, and you should have an easier time making decisions.

What Is Your Outlook?

Your outlook on underlying security refers to what you anticipate will happen to its price, such as whether you believe it will increase or decrease. These are the only two perspectives in many types of investing that can be profitable. For instance, stock traders can either buy stocks they believe will appreciate or acquire stocks they believe will depreciate; these are essentially the only two ways to benefit.

However, there are four possible outlooks for options traders to take into account: bullish (expecting the price to rise), bearish (expecting the price to fall), neutral (expecting the price not to change, or at least be reasonably constant), and volatile (expecting major price swings). This increases the number of things to consider and the number of ways to earn money.

With so many options, you can hone your perspective to make the right choice. For instance, if you have an optimistic perspective, you may further classify it as somewhat bullish (expecting a slight price increase) or extremely bullish (expecting a large price increase).

Choosing an effective plan is considerably easier when your outlook is more definite. For instance, if you anticipated that the price of an underlying investment would grow greatly, you would know not to employ a strategy that only made money on modest price increases and stopped making money if the price rose further.

Additionally, you can mix outlooks. For example, you might anticipate that the price of an underlying security will increase over time but remain stable during the short term. Alternatively, you might forecast a very consistent price while considering the possibility of a decline. There are strategies you can employ in both of those situations. These examples emphasize how adaptable options trading is while emphasizing the value of having a precise outlook and taking the appropriate actions.

As we have already indicated, when you become more familiar with the many types and begin to employ them, you will logically find it easier to select a strategy appropriate for your outlook. But you might find it harder unless you have a decent amount of experience.

Risk Vs. Reward

You must take risk management into account when deciding which tactics to employ. The risk profiles of the various strategies might differ greatly; some have predetermined maximum losses, while others have unbounded risks. Becoming familiar with risk graphs may help determine whether a risk profile matches your personal risk tolerance. The risk-to-reward ratio is another important factor because it compares the potential profit amount to the probable loss.

Single Position Or Spread Of Options?

Creating spreads is a key component of many options trading strategies since it allows you to combine many positions into one single one efficiently. Their main advantages are employing these spreads to reduce risk and lowering the initial investment required to take a position that can profit from several outcomes.

As a result, employing spreads rather than opening a single position is typically a good idea. A few benefits to taking a single position are essentially just buying or writing one kind of options contract.

First, entering a single position will cost you less in commissions than building spreads because fewer transactions are involved. This can significantly affect how profitable trades are, especially if you make many small ones. Spreads can occasionally reduce a trade's potential profitability, whereas taking a single position might result in bigger profits. Therefore, even though we believe spreads are often a better option, there may be times when a single position is a worthwhile consideration.

Mandatory Trading Levels

Your broker will assign a trading level to your account, which will, in part, dictate which you utilize. To comply with regulatory requirements and prevent their clients from taking on more risk than they should, brokers assign each account a trading level mostly based on the client's background and financial status. You can only apply some strategies with a low trading level because those that involve a lot of risk call for a greater trading level. As a result, you must undoubtedly consider this while choosing your strategy in any given circumstance.

Strategy Complexity

There are many levels of strategy complexity when it comes to trading options. There are a few that are rather straightforward, usually those that require one or two transactions. Several require three or more transactions and are also more sophisticated. You should consider a strategy's intricacy when choosing one to use because it has an impact on a variety of trading-related factors.

One reason is that you will spend more in broker commissions the more transactions you need, as we have explained earlier. You need to consider this because it can significantly impact your prospective returns, especially if you are trading on a tight budget.

It can be difficult to determine a trade's potential earnings and losses and what price fluctuations will benefit you most if you use the more complex strategies. Choosing the best entry and exit points for a position is a crucial component of trade planning, and doing so is typically much easier when employing more straightforward strategies. However, you should be aware of the additional challenges this may bring. This does not imply you should never utilize sophisticated ones because they are often the best option.

The more difficult ones also present you with an additional decision: whether to execute all necessary transactions concurrently or execute each order separately. Many online brokers have features that let you choose your strategy, and the orders it needs will then be executed automatically and simultaneously. This greatly eases daily living.

However, if you decide to use leggings, you must find the optimal location for each order and go through the procedure of placing each separately. This can make things a little more challenging, but you can increase your winnings if you can leg into and out of positions at the appropriate times.

Options Trading Strategies For Beginner

No matter how complex they are, call-and-put options are the foundation of all options strategies. Below, we have listed the five most common strategies, their return and risk breakdowns, and when a trader might use them as leverage for their upcoming investment. These strategies, however simple, can help a trader make a lot of money, but they don't come without risk. Before we start, check out these primers on call options and put options.

Long Call

By "going long" a call, the trader purchases a call in this strategy, expecting the stock price to rise over the strike price by expiration. The potential profit from this transaction is limitless, and if the stock rises, investors might make several times their initial investment.

For instance, a call option with a $20 strike price and a four-month expiration is trading at $1 for stock X, currently trading at $20 a share. One contract costs $1, each representing 100 shares, for a total cost of $100.

Risk/Reward - In this case, the strike price plus the $1 premium paid equals $21 per share, and the trader's price breaks even. For every dollar the stock increases above $20, the option's value rises by $100. The option expires worthless when the stock trades at or below the strike price.

The potential gain from a long call is essentially limitless. The call's price may rise further if the stock keeps increasing before expiration. Long calls are among the most well-liked strategies to bet on a rising stock price.

The risk of a long call is the complete loss of your investment, in this case, $100. The call will expire worthless, leaving you nothing if the stock closes less than the strike price.

When To Use - A long call is a wise alternative when you anticipate the stock will increase significantly before the option expires. The option might still be in the money if the stock climbs just slightly above the strike price, but it might not even pay back the premium, leaving you with a net loss.

Covered Call

Selling a call option is "going short" in a covered call. In this case, the trader sells a call but also purchases 100 shares of the stock that underlies the option. The short-call trade is made into a relatively secure, potentially lucrative investment by owning the stock. Traders anticipate that the stock price will be lower than the strike price at expiration. The owner must trade the stock to the call buyer at the strike price when the stock closes above the strike price.

Example: Shares of Stock X are trading at $20, and a call with a $20 strike price and a four-month expiration is trading at $1. One contract * $1 * 100 shares represented each contract, or $100, is paid as the premium. The trader spends $2,000 to purchase 100 stock shares, then earns $100 by selling one call.

Reward/Risk - In this case, the strike price minus the $1 premium paid results in the trader's break-even price of $19 per share. Below $19, the stock would lose money, more than offsetting the $1 premium, causing the trader to lose money. The trader would hold onto the stock and preserve the full premium at exactly $20. The gain is restricted at $100 over $20. The short call loses $100 for every dollar over $20, but the gain in the stock completely offsets this loss, giving the trader only the initial $100 premium as profit.

No matter how much the stock price climbs, the covered call's upside is constrained to the premium paid. More money cannot be made, but far more money can be lost. The short call entirely cancels out any profit you would have otherwise received from the stock's increase.

If the stock drops to zero, the downside is a total loss on the investment, which the premium would mitigate; if the stock declines, the covered call exposes you to a large loss. For instance, in our case, the total loss would be $1,900 if the stock dropped to zero.

When To Use - If you already own the stock and don't anticipate it to climb considerably very soon, a covered call can be an excellent way to make money. Thus, the strategy allows you to turn your current possessions into a cash stream. It can be helpful in tax-advantaged accounts where you might otherwise have to pay taxes on the premium and capital profits if the stock is called. Covered calls are popular with older investors who need the income.

Long Put

In this approach, the trader purchases a put, often known as a "going long" put, expecting the stock price to be lower at expiration than the strike price. If the stock declines dramatically, the potential profit on this transaction could be many times the initial investment.

For instance, a put with a $20 strike price and a four-month expiration is trading at $1 for stock X, currently trading at $20 a share. One contract costs $1, each representing 100 shares, for a total cost of $100.

Risk/Reward - In this case, the put is profitable if the stock closes at $19 per share at option expiration, which is the strike price less the $1 premium. Every dollar the stock falls below $20, the put's value rises by $100. The put expires worthless above $20, and the trader forfeits the $100 premium.

Because the gain can exceed the cost of the option premium, the potential upside on a long put is virtually as good as that on a long call. A stock's upside is limited by the fact that it can never go below zero, whereas the upside of a long call is potentially limitless. A safer alternative to shorting a stock is to use long puts, another straightforward and well-liked strategy to bet on the stock's collapse.

The highest loss on a long put is the premium, which is $100. The put expires worthless, and you lose your investment if the stock closes higher than the strike price at the time of the option's expiration.

When To Use - A long put is a wise investment when you anticipate that the stock will decline significantly before the option expires. The option will be in the money if the stock drops just slightly below the strike price, but it might not pay back the premium, leaving you with a net loss.

Short Put

This strategy is the opposite of the long put; however, in this case, the trader sells a put (known as "going short" a put) and anticipates that the stock price will exceed the strike price by the time the put expires. The maximum a short put can earn is a cash premium, which the trader receives in exchange for selling. The trader must purchase the shares at the strike price if it closes below it at option expiration.

Example: Shares of Stock X are trading at $20 each, and a put with a $20 strike price and a four-month expiration is trading for $1. One contract * $1 * 100 shares represented each contract, or $100, is paid as the premium.

Risk/Reward - In this case, the short put equals $19 (the strike price less the premium received) or breaks even. For every dollar the price declines below $19, the short put costs the trader $100, while above $20, the put seller receives the full $100 premium. The put seller would receive a portion of the premium, but not all, between $19 and $20.

The short put's potential gain is always limited to the premium paid, in this case, $100. The highest return on a short put is the amount paid to the seller up front, much like with a short or covered call.

If the price fell to zero, the downside of a short put would be equal to the total value of the underlying stock less the premium received. In this case, the trader would have to invest $2,000 in the company (100 shares * $20 strike price), but the $100 premium gained would negate this cost, resulting in a loss of $1,900 overall.

When To Use - A short put is the right course of action when you anticipate that the stock will close at the strike price or higher at the option's expiration. For the option to expire worthless and allow you to keep the entire premium paid, the stock must be at or above the strike price.

If the stock is put to you, your broker will want to ensure you have enough equity in your account to purchase it. If the put expires in the money, many traders will have enough cash or margin in their accounts to buy the stock. Without purchasing the stock directly, it is easy to close out the options position before it expires and take the loss.

Longer-term investors who would want to buy the stock at the strike price and receive some extra money in return for doing so may also find this technique beneficial.

Married Put

This strategy is similar to the long put with a twist. The trader purchases a put in addition to owning the underlying stock. This is a hedged trade in which the trader anticipates a rise in the stock but seeks "insurance" if it declines. The long put counters any potential reduction in the stock price.

For instance, a put with a $20 strike price and a four-month expiration is trading at $1 for stock X, currently trading at $20 a share. One contract costs $1, each representing 100 shares, for a total cost of $100. For $2,000, the trader purchases 100 shares of stock and one put.

Risk/Reward - In this case, the married put breaks even at $21, the strike price plus the $1 premium expense. Under $20, the long put cancels out the stock's loss dollar for dollar. Even though the put expires worthless and the trader loses the premium paid, in this case, $100, the total profit grows by $100 for every dollar the stock increases over $21.

In theory, the married put's maximum upside is limitless, less the put's cost, so long as the stock price keeps increasing. The premium is what it costs to insure the stock and provide it the chance to rise with little risk because the married put is in a hedged position.

The cost of the premium is the married put's drawback. The put gains value as the value of the stock holding decreases, matching the loss dollar for dollar. Due to this hedge, the trader suffers the smaller option cost loss as opposed to the larger stock loss.

When To Use - When you believe a stock's price will increase greatly before the option expires but also risk falling significantly, a married put may be a wise investment. The married put enables you to keep the stock and benefit from possible gains if it increases while still being protected from a substantial loss if it decreases. For instance, a trader who wishes to be covered may anticipate news, such as earnings, that could move the stock up or down.

Chapter Six

Trading Options On Stocks

Knowing the different trading strategies that may be used to make the most profit is important because the stock market is becoming more difficult to navigate daily. Today's traders must understand that to maximize their profits from their trades; they need to be aware of the many strategies used by specialists rather than seizing the first opportunity they come across. These strategies can reduce risk and increase earnings. Traders can learn how to benefit from any stock's flexibility with some work.

Here, we list the greatest option trading strategies for people to try. Your trading style will determine whether you choose to apply these strategies, but at the very least, if you know how they work, you will be more prepared to adjust to shifting market conditions.

Bullish Option Trading Strategies

Let's look at some Bullish Options Trading Strategies first.

Bull Call Spread

The Debt Spreads subcategory of Options Trading Strategies includes Bull Call Spread. Consider buying a call option for a lower-risk bullish bet if you are bullish on a company or ETF but do not want to risk buying shares altogether.

Meanwhile, Call Options can be expensive and expose you to higher risk than you are used to. Perhaps you're thinking, "Is there another way?" Yes, that is the response. To lower your initial cost and risk, you could buy a Bull Call Spread.

In the Bull Call Spread option, you can still purchase the long call option that expresses your bullish viewpoints, but you can offset some of that price by selling a short call option that is opposed to it, reducing your risk.

You can create a bull call spread by buying one call option and selling another with the same expiration date but a lower cost and higher strike price. This approach is also regarded as the best one for selling options.

Bull Put Spread

The Bull Put Spread Options Trading Strategy is employed by options traders who predict that the underlying asset's price will rise gradually. This option typically belongs to the Credit Spreads group. The buying and selling of puts and calls are more involved than that, despite this options trading strategy not being the most complex.

In other words, this spread consists of selling and purchasing a put option with a lesser strike. Theta decay would profit you in this scenario, given that the Short-Put Option will lose value more quickly than your Long-Put Option position.

In this situation, executing a Bull Put Position would be preferable because theta decay causes such a position to appreciate rapidly every day. This method is regarded as an excellent option purchasing strategy.

Bull Call Ratio Backspread

A trader must have a strong positive bias toward the stock to place this trade. Being just a little bit bullish won't help with this trade. One peculiarity of the Bull Call Ratio Backspread is that the highest loss occurs in the direction the trader expects the trade to progress.

The Bull Call Ratio Backspread is one bullish strategy that could be employed instead of only buying call options. Selling one or more at-the-money or out-of-the-money calls and buying two or three calls longer in the money than the call sold to make up the Call Ratio Backspread. This tactic is also regarded as the finest one for selling options.

Synthetic Call

An investor buys and holds shares to begin a synthetic call, otherwise known as a synthetic long call. The investor also purchases an at-the-money put option on the same shares as insurance against a drop in the stock's value.

Many investors think of this method as an insurance policy against the stock dropping significantly while they are still holding the shares.

Bearish Option Trading Strategies

The trading strategies for bearish options are as follows:

Bear Call Spread

A double options trading method known as a Bear Call Spread may be used if one's outlook on the market is unfavorable.

By employing this strategy, a trader will sell a shorter-term call option while concurrently purchasing a longer-term call option with a higher strike price and the same underlying asset and expiration date. One obtains a net profit by obtaining a bigger option premium on the call sold than the cost purchased.

Bear Put Spread

When a trader or investor believes that the price of a security or asset will drop slightly, they will use a bear put spread. A Bear Put Spread is created by purchasing Put Options and selling an equal number of Puts on similar assets with the same expiry date and a low target price.

The highest profit a trader may achieve with this approach is the difference between these two strike prices, less the entire cost of the options.

Strip

An optimistic investor on volatility and pessimistic on the market's direction must use the Strip Strategy. This approach involves buying two lots of "At-the-Money Put Options" and "At-the-Money Call Options." Both alternatives must use the same underlying security and expiration month. A bearish form of the Strip is identical to the standard Long Straddle.

When the underlying makes a substantial move at expiration, moving more favorably toward loss, the Strip Strategy may produce significant winnings.

Synthetic Put

It is risk-equivalent to buying a Put option for an investor to sell short a stock and buy a call.

By owning both a long call option and a short stock position on the same stock, this option strategy resembles a long-put option. In a word, it's a strategy that traders might use if they have a bearish wager on stock but are worried about its likelihood of showing near-term strength.

Assessing Opportunities In Various Sectors

It's time to start planning how you'll identify trading chances at this point. Even if you are completely knowledgeable about options trading, your knowledge will be useless until you can put it all into practice and spot profitable trading opportunities.

Even though options trading is extremely complicated, anyone willing to put in the effort to master the subject can eventually succeed. However, simply understanding how to trade options is insufficient; you must also understand how to profit from it. You will need to make the necessary effort to identify the right possibilities and then make the proper transactions; thus, this requires hard work and dedication.

If you can accomplish that regularly, your goals will likely be realized. This page examines how to find potentially successful options trading chances.

Which Underlying Assets?

Although options contracts are assets in and of themselves, they are derivatives whose value is derived from the underlying assets to which they are related. Stocks, foreign currencies, commodities, and indexes are just a few examples of the many underlying assets that can be used to buy and sell options contracts.

Options trading is a particularly flexible type of investing since you can invest in various financial instruments simply by buying and selling options contracts. Choosing which financial instruments to include should be one of your first considerations when looking for prospective possibilities to trade options.

It should be made clear that you are not required to choose to trade only stock, currency, or index options. You are free to buy and sell as many options as you choose. You do, however, need to consider how you'll research potential transactions and how you'll find relevant possibilities.

Given the variety of options, you would have the best chance of discovering chances if you elected to take into account a variety of different underlying securities. However, you would need to be ready to invest a lot of time in researching various financial markets, which could make it difficult for you to find as many possibilities as you would like.

Alternately, if you decided to exclusively trade stock options based on stocks in a particular industry, you could narrow your study to only publicly traded businesses involved in that industry. You might become an authority in that area and, using your knowledge, become much better at seeing possibilities relating to it.

Of course, the disadvantage of adopting such a constrained strategy is that you might pass up many other opportunities in various industries and marketplaces you aren't even considering.

There isn't a perfect way to go about this element of looking for possibilities, so we can't offer any advice on that front. It's up to you to choose what you feel comfortable with and what you believe will provide you with the best chance of success, but all we ask is that you take the time to think about the underlying assets you want to include.

Using your expertise in a specific industry or market makes sense if you have it, but there is nothing wrong with adopting a broader perspective. You may choose to study the price changes of the options contracts and trade appropriately rather than investigating and analyzing the underlying assets of options.

Making Research

The emergence of online technology and intent has had various effects on trading and investing. Online brokers were created, as a result, greatly simplifying the process of purchasing and selling financial instruments. Financial instrument information is also now much more widely available.

Investors benefit from the nearly endless supply of information available on the internet for research reasons. It is imperative to check the exchanges to obtain the most recent quotes and keep up with global events that may impact the markets. It is crucial to obtain financial data from publicly traded corporations. The internet is a fantastic information resource full of figures, facts, and statistics.

Of course, conducting research for trading goals involves more than just acquiring information. The actual expertise is knowing what information to seek and how to interpret it. Even though it is a skill in and of itself, this skill may be readily improved over time with lots of practice.

When identifying potentially lucrative prospects, you will give yourself a far better chance of success if you are willing to invest a reasonable amount of time in conducting research and assessing what you discover.

Technical & Fundamental Analysis

As explained in previous chapters, the two primary tools traders and investors use to assess data and choose which trades and investments to make are fundamental and technical analysis. Despite serving essentially the same function, they serve that purpose in quite different ways.

Fundamental analysis generally entails gathering as much data as possible about certain security and then analyzing it to ascertain its underlying value and how it relates to its trading price.

For instance, if you wanted to perform a fundamental analysis on a stock in a specific company, you would look at various factors, including the company's current financial strength, earnings reports, the caliber of its management team, and its competitive edge in the market. By doing this, you could determine whether the stock was fairly valued compared to its underlying value or overvalued. Although it is oversimplified, this illustrates how fundamental analysis is put to use.

The foundation of technical analysis is using historical data to forecast future moves. It entails looking for patterns in price and volume charts and graphs to identify trends likely to be repeated. According to the hypothesis, by observing these tendencies, you can accurately predict how the price of a security will change over a specific period. Even though this is a rather oversimplified version of technical analysis, it provides a basic summary of the process.

Investors normally utilize fundamental and technical analyses when purchasing stocks, but they can also be useful when purchasing options. The basic concept is that you would utilize these techniques to understand how you anticipate the price of financial instruments to change and then trade the proper options contracts to profit from those moves.

Since there are many factors to examine, neither fundamental nor technical analysis can be regarded as superior to the other. In some ways, it boils down to personal taste; if you are more adept at or more at ease utilizing one of the strategies for your study, it makes sense to choose that strategy. You might find it more convenient to combine the two or to utilize fundamental analysis in some cases and technical analysis in others.

But it's important to remember that, more often than not, options trading is about profiting from swift price changes. Fundamental analysis can assist you in understanding a security's intrinsic value, and long-term investors often use it to buy inexpensive equities that are expected to increase in value over time. It doesn't, however, always make it easier to forecast short-term price changes.

Technical analysis can, which is why options traders will likely benefit more from adopting it. This is especially true for day traders making numerous short-term daily transactions.

When finding possible transactions, you should also consider the amount of capital needed and the level of risk.

Chapter Seven

Managing Risk In Options Trading

First things first: What is risk management in options trading? This is the process of minimizing financial risk in your trading strategy by any means necessary. Each trader will manage risk differently. You must consider your risk tolerance to create a risk management strategy that will work. More aggressive traders can manage risk, although they won't control risk as much as conservative traders.

It's crucial to understand that minimizing risk does result in a lesser possibility for profit. This is because many strategies you'll utilize include hedging your trades and exercising options early to benefit. A more aggressive trader may incur greater risk but also reap greater rewards. To begin with any investment strategy, it's crucial to take the time to create a trading plan that matches your risk tolerance.

Why Learning How To Manage Risk For Stock Options Is So Important

Aiming to maximize earnings is important, but learning how to manage risk for stock options may be more crucial. Why? Because continuously winning trades, no matter how small, results in higher overall returns than winning a few large trades while losing the majority.

Consider this: wouldn't you appreciate a stress-free trading approach that consistently nets you a 5–10% return on investment with every trade you make? Sure, the thrill of a home run is unbeatable. But over time, those singles pile up. Small, regular returns are preferable to high, irregular returns with plenty of losses. The best thing, though? You can still make a staggering profit with a successful risk management approach.

5 Tips & Tricks For Managing Risk When Trading Stock Options

Are you prepared to understand how to control risk when trading stock options? There are numerous strategies to enjoy large rewards while minimizing your risk. We will outline our top options risk management strategies below, covering everything from using correct analysis to hedging your bets.

1. Spend Some Time Learning About Options Trading First!

We are aware that you are eager to begin trading options. However, if you have no prior experience, start by trading options on paper. Paper trading simulates actual trading activities using fictitious funds. Before spending your hard-earned money, you can feel things and understand the highs and lows of trading. It is risky in and of itself to jump into options trading without first taking the time to build experience and confidence.

2. Take Profits

It can be enticing to keep waiting to collect extra earnings when an option contract is in the money early on. However, we advise you to use your options and to cash in on profits when you can. Let's say you buy an options contract from firm XYZ. According to the rules, your strike price is set at $10 per share with a six-month exercise date for 100 shares. The underlying stock price has increased to $14 after one month. If you exercise your option, you'll make $400 immediately.

But hold on—according to your technical analysis, the price may continue its upward path. Should you wait to extract an additional 1% to 2%? Sure, but you'll kick yourself if you miss the opportunity and the price changes before you can exercise the option. Here is a more effective method for trading options that enables you to collect earnings right away while leaving room for potential future gains:

Assuming the example above is for a call option; you can now purchase those shares at the $10 strike price. Then, you can sell a portion of your shares at the $14 market price for quick cash. Then, when the price rises, keep retaining the remainder of your shares and gradually sell them off. Are you still holding the final 15% of your investment, and the price reverses? You are still in the black because you have taken profits until now. One of the best methods to manage risk with any trading strategy, including options, is to engage in what is known as selling into strength.

3. Eliminate Losses

We want to talk about the flip side of the coin, which is capping your losses when taking profits. Nobody wants to make a trade and lose money. Even if losses are rare, it is crucial to keep them in check. Even if most of your trades are profitable, you will still be in a deficit. Over a week, a month, or a year, you can still keep a good ROI on your capital by taking your medication and being willing to take minor losses sometimes.

It's crucial to discuss time decay when it comes to trading options contracts in particular. Time decay is the term used to describe how your contract's value decreases over each day. Remember that your options contract is null and invalid after the exercise date. Additionally, as the exercise date draws nearer, time decay causes your contract's value to decrease. Regardless of whether you have money or not, this is true.

Fortunately, the most you can lose on an options contract is the premium you paid to buy the contract. Options contracts are a wonderful value investment for traders because they are often rather affordable. If you don't intend to exercise your options, you have two options: let the contract expire or sell it back on the stock market. Speculative investors could buy your contract and assist you in covering some losses, even if you might not receive the full value you paid for the contract.

4. Diversify

You've probably heard of diversification if you've learned about investing. Putting all eggs in one basket will indeed guarantee failure. Therefore, when looking for options contracts to trade, diversify your portfolio by considering various industries, businesses, and options contract types.

We should also discuss position size at this point. One thing you want to avoid is losing everything by blowing up your trading account. As a result, keep your position sizes to a reasonable portion of your working capital. Going all-in on an easy victory might be very alluring, but you should resist investing more than 20% of your capital in any contract. This reduces risk and makes sure you have money on hand to invest in other possibilities that may arise.

5. Purchase Reliable Stock Prediction Software

The best method to control risk in options trading or any other type of investing is to succeed in every deal you do. Not difficult. This is, unfortunately, not realistic. However, investing in a trustworthy, tried-and-true stock forecasting program will give you the best chance of success. But how precisely would this assist you in risk management?

As a result of the insights the program gives you, you'll be able to buy contracts with more assurance. Even better, you can eliminate any ambiguity over when to acquire your contract or exercise your options. How? They offer a clear buy, sell, or hold recommendation for any given stock. A free stock analysis will show you how this works in practice.

Using stock forecasting software to invest can help you manage risk better and win more deals. Simple indications enable you to evaluate opportunities and enter or exit the market at the ideal moment.

Trading Psychology And Emotional Discipline

Without prior direct investing experience, it might be challenging to understand trading psychology fully. Most traders know the importance of adopting and maintaining the proper mentality. The short-term trader will find this to be especially true. Making quick decisions on short notice will be necessary if you are day trading the markets, and they could mean the difference between winning and losing trade. The ability to adhere to a previously set plan where you are confident in booking profits and enforcing a stop loss is also required. Making time-sensitive trading decisions requires you to keep your emotions in check.

The most common feelings that traders go through include fear, anxiety, conviction, enthusiasm, greed, and overconfidence.

Fear/Anxiety

Trading too large is a common source of concern. Trading at the wrong size unnecessarily increases volatility and lets you make mistakes you otherwise wouldn't make if you weren't under the pressure of potentially suffering more losses than usual.

Another reason for your fear (or anxiety) is that you are in the "wrong" trade, which doesn't suit your trading plan.

Conviction/Excitement

The two main emotions you'll want to feed off are conviction and excitement, and you should experience these feelings in every trade you make. Conviction is the icing on the cake of each successful transaction; therefore, chances are excellent that you aren't in the "right" deal for you if you lack either of these emotions.

By "right," we mean the transaction that complies with your trading strategy. Both profitable and unsuccessful trades have the potential to be losers. To keep yourself winning and losing on just profitable investments is the goal. This can be ensured by ensuring you are confident in a particular trade.

Greed/Overconfidence

You can grow greedy if you only want to make transactions you believe are highly likely to succeed. Although your greed may have resulted from your success, you could fall and experience a downturn if you aren't careful.

Ensure your trade mechanics are sound, including keeping to stops, targets, adequate risk/management, and sound trade setups. Overconfident traders who make poor decisions can halt a successful streak.

How To Improve Discipline And Control Emotions While Trading

Planning your strategy is essential if you want to keep negative emotions out of your trade. In financial markets, the proverb "Failing to plan is planning to fail" might be true.

There are numerous ways to succeed as a trader. Some numerous ways and strategies might support traders in achieving their goals. But rather than being based on "hunches," whatever will work for that person will often be a defined and systematic strategy.

Here are some strategies to help you feel more in control of your feelings while trading.

Make Your Own Rules

You can better manage your emotions by creating your own rules for trading. Setting profit targets, stopping losses, and risk/reward tolerance criteria for entering and exiting trades may be part of your trading rules.

Trade In The Appropriate Market Context

Keeping away from less-than-ideal market situations is also wise. It's a good idea to avoid trading when you're not "feeling" it. Don't depend on the market to make you feel better; if trading isn't for you, the best action might be to stop doing it.

Self-Control, Not Money

Even though it sounds absurd, the first thing to do when entering the trading world is to put money aside. You might wonder how that is feasible. Trading is all about money. True and false. Each trader's ultimate goal is to use speculation to amass as much riches as possible. However, you must focus on things that produce money rather than the money itself to reach your goal. Start formulating trading plans and tactics; if you follow these steps correctly, you will see money coming in.

Somebody Is Watching

Here is another tactic that you might find useful. Both seasoned traders and newcomers can use it. And what's the best? Applying is quite simple. If you've heard of well-known traders, consider the one you admire the most. If not, look up some well-known traders and choose one. The secret is to gain some knowledge of his traits, manner of trade, and successes. Learn as much as you can about this individual.

On to the next action. Imagine that this man is behind you while you are trading. This man can see everything and judge you based on every trade you open and every dollar you invest. By doing this, you'll improve your self-control and cut down on your distracted time.

Write A List

Everything that is connected to your trading operations in any manner should be noted down. What assets do you trade? When do you make a trade? The reason you trade. Make a list of specific, simple-to-understand goals and a timetable for achieving them. Print out the entire document (it should only take up one page), then hang it where you can see it while trading. When in doubt, glance at the document to refresh your memory on the overall situation. You can keep up with other traders with a clear strategy and set goals.

A-Day Rule

Commit to maintaining your discipline for only one day. "Today, I will follow my established guidelines and avoid engaging in emotional trading." That's all it takes. The majority of artists employ the same method. They tell themselves to sit down and draw one straight line when they are depressed and unable to practice. It won't be the only line when you're ready to practice. The second line follows the first, and you soon find yourself devoting several hours. Maintain your discipline not only for one day but every day. You'll soon discover that maintaining discipline is much easier and has become second nature.

Create A Trading Strategy And A Trading Journal

Planning for several outcomes in the lead-up to major news events may also be a strategy to consider underlying factors.

The difference in performance between novice traders who use a trading plan and those who don't can be significant. The first step in combating trading emotions is to put together a trading plan, but unfortunately, this will not mitigate the consequences of these emotions. Keeping a journal for your options trading may be beneficial.

Relax!

You'll be more able to react logically to changes in the market if you're at ease and like your trading.

Conclusion

Hopefully, you can decide if options are better for you with less difficulty now that you are familiar with the options, their two different types (calls and puts), and their risk level.

The most crucial lesson is that you should know what you're getting into in advance, even though you might be anxious to join the options bandwagon.

Options provide many ways for investors to make money by trading the underlying securities. Different combinations of options, underlying assets, and other derivatives can be used in several different methods. Buying calls, buying puts, selling covered calls, and purchasing protected puts are fundamental strategies for newcomers. Options trading has benefits over trading actual assets, such as downside protection and leveraged returns, but it also has drawbacks, such as the need to pay the premium in advance.